# BEST 50

## Clean Eating
## Salad Recipes
## For Quick Weight Loss
## & Detox

**Table of Content:**

## What is Clean Eating?

Clean eating basically means eating foods closest to their most natural and whole form that is free of additives, preservatives or anything artificial. With a clean diet you want to consume foods that are minimally treated, if treated at all. The concept is that food must not come from a box, package, mix or bag. Therefore, food comes from nature and not from a business. If you make a purchase of prepackaged foods, then it should have minimal ingredients, and you should be able to pronounce them. A good rule of thumb is that the more ingredients a food has the less pure it is.

Although it may seem to be just another fad diet, "clean eating" is actually a philosophy that motivates people to become aware of the foods we eat. The central principle is to cut out all the processed foods and use whole and unadulterated foods such as vegetables, fruits, legumes and whole grains instead. Some clean eaters even eliminate dairy and / or meat.

**Why go clean?**

Because it's more of a lifestyle approach than a controlled diet program, clean eating attracts people who want to clean up their diet without counting calories, fats and carbs. Of course, there is often a weight loss benefit. Many studies have shown a link between eating processed foods and obesity.

What's more, evidence suggests that eating clean can make people feel healthier and more energetic, so they're less likely to go back to eating foods that are processed. With more energy comes a leaner and healthier body.

**Basics of eating clean:**

Drink lots of water

Most of us do not get enough water, and often confuse our water needs for hunger. When that happens, we start eating even when we are not hungry.

Reduce or eliminate low fat, light, reduced fat, or any other processed food.

When companies remove the fat and calories from the food, they need to fill it with chemicals, additives or fillers to keep the same taste and texture. Using real ingredients is better for you and always tastes better.

Eat whole grains and stay away from or limit the amount of refined white flour you use.

If you are unsure if it is really a whole grain food, just read the label. Bread that is whole grain will have whole grain as its first ingredient. Same is with the pasta. A lot of bread and pasta are dressed with healthy packaging, but if you read the label, you will know that they are not better than their refined counterparts. Do not forget brown rice, bulgur, quinoa and other whole grains - they are nutritious, filling and cheap!

Eat beans, nuts and seeds.

All these are packed with nutrients and are very affordable. Of course, be careful with the salt and sugar.

Eat plenty of fruits and vegetables.

Try to buy organic when you can, but if you cannot then do not worry because eating more fruits and vegetables is always better than not, just make sure you wash them thoroughly. If you do not have access to fresh local fruits and vegetables all year round then head to the freezer section. You can find plenty of reasonably priced organic fruits and vegetables, hiding out there.

Eat wild fish and organic grass-fed man-raised beef, chicken and other meats.

I know it can be expensive, but in my opinion this is an area I do not mind spending the extra money. It tastes better, is more nutritious and is generally better for the environment.

Reduce or eliminate the sugar.

My honest advice is to give up sugar completely, try to keep it under control as much as you can and replace it with healthy options (liquid stevia, maple syrup and honey). Do not use artificial sweeteners of any kind. Again, if it is artificial and not natural, I do not usually eat it.

Eliminate fast food.

I do not believe in eating at fast food chains as they do not offer any nutritional value. These food chains are in the business of making more money and not making you a healthier person.

# The Amazing Powers of Eating Healthy Salads for Quick and Effective Weight Loss

If one of your goals is to shed those extra pounds as soon as you can, than incorporating salads into your healthy clean menus could be the solution. In fact salads are a full meal enhanced with proteins like chicken or fish and they are an excellent choice for your diet since they contain plenty of nutrients, vitamins and minerals. Pretty much all your body needs to stay healthy and slim is found inside a good healthy salad and it is a very light meal that you can enjoy any time during the day. You certainly will feel better and lighter when you eat a salad full of greens than when you eat those heavy and intoxicating processed foods.

The main components of salads are veggies and leafy greens and sometimes fresh fruits that make this very special dish the perfect tool for your weight loss purposes. Eating salads is not only great to lose weight fast but it is also very good for your overall health. Fibrous carbs will be entering your system when you make salads a part of your daily diet. This is the perfect type of meal to fight hunger attacks and fill full at the same time. You feel refreshed when you eat salads and this is mainly because of their mayor components, the veggies are full of water, dietary fiber and low in calories.

Eating salads that contain broccoli and other green ingredients makes a huge difference in how your body looks and feels since you won´t be filling your system with empty starchy carbohydrates that only make you fat. Salads provide multiple nutrients that in combination with healthy proteins will make a perfect diet to maintain a slim and strong body all the time. There is no need to practice unhealthy hunger tactics with a salad based diet. You just have to eat them frequently to maintain your metabolic rate active and working at all times so you burn all the unwanted fat fast. The key is to eat a healthy salad meal at least 5 to six times per day.

Once you´ve lost the unwanted weight it is a matter of maintaining your slim figure by making salads a main part of your healthy menus. You can make your salads as tasty as you want. Inside this book you will find the best collection of healthy clean eating salads to accomplish your weight loss goals in a short period of time with great flavor and with high nutritious value while you detox your body at the same time. Don´t forget to drink lots of pure H2O with your salads so your digestive system works properly and your body gets rid of all the unwanted toxins that are making you fat and sluggish.

For your weight loss purposes keep the balance between the added proteins to your salads and your green ingredients, make sure that you add at least 20 to 30 g of protein so your metabolism doesn´t slows down and you don´t lose muscle body mass. A healthy snack can be just an all veggie salad without the protein component so you are able to get by without hunger during your day.

For a fast weight loss, stick to the lower calorie salads and stay below the 1200 calories per day until you reach your desired goal. After that maintaining a slim figure is very easy if you continue with a healthy balanced menu that incorporates healthy salads. Eating salads is an easy, fast and fun way of nourishing your system that only requires from you the commitment to change your eating habits and start enjoying the tasty natural flavors that they have for your health. So start with your with clean eating diet now!

# Clean Eating Benefits for Your Body and Health

While many generations, individuals and movements take credit for playing a key part in bringing clean eating to the world, the truth is that clean eating has its roots in every ancient tradition that appreciates the earth, the food, and the human body.

The original goal was to consume food in the form closest to its natural state, while eliminating toxic substances present in artificial ingredients. The clean lifestyle has gone through changes and improvements through the years as new health information became available, but it still offers the original goals and beliefs today as it did at the start.

Even though clean eating promotes healthy functioning of all the systems of the body, the benefits are far greater than just an improvement in how you feel. The following are some of the other benefits you get when you start eating clean.

## Faster Metabolism

Consuming smaller meals every two or three hours gives your body the constant fuel it needs. This eating schedule solves one of the most common queries that dieters have: not really feeling full following a meal. With clean eating, your food cravings and hunger tend to be satisfied by the smaller sized doses of scrumptious food. When you eat every two or three hours, your body just doesn't run out of gas. When people go hungry for very long periods without eating (hours or even an entire day), they suffer from fatigue and lack of mental focus. Both are serious consequences associated with frequent blood sugar drops.

By eating smaller meals six times a day, you speed up your metabolism and your body is able to utilize the complex carbohydrates, healthy proteins and healthy fat as fuel rather than storing them when preparing for another long stretch without food. Using energy instead of storing it means you will be able to reduce your body fat while increasing muscle mass. The clean salad recipes presented in this book are an ideal tool for achieving a faster metabolic rate while you eat frequently during the day. These recipes are clean and have plenty of nutrients, not empty calories.

## Improved brain function

When pure foods replace the toxic, nutrient-lacking foods, some of the first noticeable improvements you see are increase in energy levels and mental clarity. "Unclean" foods come with long list of ingredients that are even hard-to-pronounce. These artificial and processed foods have little if any natural substance, as well as lack in essential nutrients and vitamins. They cause hormonal imbalances and offer little in terms of nutrition that promotes vitality.

The good news is that by replacing unhealthy foods that ruin the body's systems with natural whole foods like healthy salads, all the body's systems come back in line with peak performance in no time! That means more energy, less fatigue and sluggishness, much better ability to focus, and improved memory and brain function. . . and who'd not want all that?

## Enhanced Performance and Recovery

Although performance and recovery may seem important only for athletes, health and fitness enthusiasts and body builders, the body's ability to perform at its best and recover most effectively should matter for everyone. Whether you are practicing a triathlon or simply taking leisurely walks with your dog every day, your body needs to have the proper nutrition to perform various tasks. Eating these healthy and clean salad recipes is the formula you need to start losing weight and feeling more energized.

Proper nutrition for good performance and recovery is a combination of complex carbohydrates, lean proteins, and fats. Clean eating promotes a combination of these three foods at every meal, so that your body has the right nutrients accessible when needed without having to plan.

**Better Hydration**

Water is a constant multi-tasker in your body. It acts as a detoxing agent, the clean fuel, and a rejuvenating comfort for organs and the skin. Water also plays a role in flushing out harmful toxins necessary to get your body back on track. Salads contain a great proportion of water and every salad meal should ideally be complemented with a good and generous glass of this precious liquid from nature. This will improve your digestion and stimulate your bowel movements naturally so you lose weight and stay slim.

Replacing sugary drinks and sodas with water is one of the most important things you can do to clean your diet. With constant hydration, your body will no longer suffer from dehydration, headache, fatigue, and the false hunger pains that make you munch a sweet snack instead of a glass of water. Last, and surely not least, water has absolutely no calories, so it does not matter how much you drink. . . Your body can only drop excess weight rather than gain it!

Nowadays, we know more about the importance of a clean diet than what we knew ten, twenty or fifty years back. We have learned about the harmful effects of sugar, fats, refined products, and other ingredients (synthetic and otherwise) when consumed in excess. Numerous studies have shown that removing these ingredients from your diet helps in preventing illness and disease whilst improving your health and vitality. What this means for your health is a stronger and leaner body that is detoxified and ready for an active life.

# Why You Have to Stay Away from Processed Foods

If you want to be as healthy as possible and experience greatly increased energy and vibrancy then one of the most important changes you can make is to eliminate processed foods from your diet as much as you can. Processed foods have many seriously undesirable properties from a nutritional standpoint. Their prevalence in the standard Western diet is one of the main reasons why the incidence rates of cancer, diabetes and obesity are at an all-time high and, sadly, continue to get worse. Fortunately by eliminating processed foods from your diet you can buck the trend of these worrying statistics and live a life of optimum health and vitality, especially when you incorporate some of our healthy alternatives like the healthy salad recipes found in this book.

## Full of Preservatives and Additives

Virtually every processed food contains high levels of preservatives and additives. The manufacturing process behind the production of the thousands of processed foods you see on supermarket shelves every single day virtually always requires preservatives to be added in order for the shelf life of the food to be as long as possible. This can be confirmed by just a cursory glance at the food label of any common processed foods such as spam, fish sticks or hot dogs. The majorities of preservatives used are unnatural and even those which are natural, such as salt, are certainly not desirable to be consumed in any great quantity on a daily basis. To make the processed foods more palatable to consumers the manufacturers add in any number of the hundreds of different man-made additives available to them, even including those which have mounting and damning evidence against them in terms of their effects on human health such MSG and Aspartame. Even more incredibly, a great number of processed foods have additives added merely to change their color and make them more attractive. All in all it is clear that for this reason alone processed foods have no rightful place in the human diet.

## High Levels of Trans Fats

One of the most alarming things about processed foods is the sky high levels of trans fats that most of them contain. They are convenient to the manufacturer as they allow them to extend the shelf life of the food and keep their costs low; however, to the consumer, they can have a devastating long-term health impact which may include greatly increasing the chances of having a heart attack or stroke due to the increase in bad cholesterol levels that they frequently cause.

## Not What Humans are supposed to Eat

Processed foods are a very recent phenomenon when compared with the human body which evolved over a long period of time. Natural food sources - such as fresh proteins, nuts and vegetables - are what our body is designed to eat and, therefore, your body doesn't take kindly to being pumped full of the synthetic additives, denatured structure and empty calories contained in processed foods. Most of the common ailments that plague millions of people in our society including fibromyalgia, chronic fatigue, acne, depression (to name just a few) have processed food and the human body's inability to deal with it at the very root of the problem.

## What Should You Eat Instead?

Now that you are clearly aware of the terrible health consequences of consuming a diet full of processed foods it is important to look at the alternatives available. First and foremost, try to include organic, locally grown produce that is in its natural state, in as large a percentage of your diet as possible. Aim to eat between 5 and 10 portions of fruit and vegetables on daily basis and try to eat them raw as this keeps the intrinsic vitamin, mineral and nutrient content in the most helpful form for the human body rather than becoming denatured through cooking. Steam fish and naturally fed white chicken breast at least 3 times a week to ensure you get adequate protein for muscle growth and repair as well as consuming healthy fats such as walnut and olive oil. Over time you will get used to this more natural way of eating and have no desire to return to eating damaging processed foods which can so detrimentally harm your health. Salads are just the perfect meal where you can get all this components in a healthy, tasty and delicious way.

# Collection of the Best 50 Clean Salad Recipes

## 1. Super Healthy Salmon Salad with Cherry Tomatoes and Spinach

Makes: 4 servings

**Ingredients**:

- Five cups of organic baby spinach leaves
- 1 package (7.1 oz.) of skinless & boneless pink salmon
- 1 cup of cherry tomatoes, halved
- Two tbsp. extra virgin olive oil
- Two tbsp. of balsamic vinegar
- 1/2 teaspoon kosher salt

- Freshly ground black pepper

**Method**:

Mix all components in a large bowl.

Toss well to combine and serve. Enjoy!

Nutrition facts per serving: 219 calories - 21g protein - 6g carbohydrate - 12g fat (2g saturated) - 2g fiber

## 2. Super Healthy Salmon and Spinach Salad with Hard-Boiled Egg

Serves: 4

**Ingredients**:

- Five cups baby spinach
- 4 ounces cooked salmon fillets, flaked
- Two hard-boiled eggs, peeled and chopped
- 2 tbsp. of extra virgin olive oil
- 2 tbsp. of freshly squeezed lemon juice
- 1/2 tbsp. sea salt
- Freshly ground black pepper

Mix all of the ingredients in a bowl, and toss well to combine.

Serve and enjoy!

---

Nutrition facts per serving: 166 calories, 11g protein, 4g carbohydrate, 12g fat (2g saturated), 1g fiber

---

## 3. Delicious and Healthy Copped Mediterranean Salad

**Ingredients:**

- 1 pkg (9 oz each) romaine lettuce, coarsely chopped
- Two cups of chopped tomatoes with Basil, Garlic and Oregano, drained
- 2 cups of garbanzo beans, drained and rinsed
- ½ cup of black olives, drained
- 2/3 cup crumbled feta cheese
- 1/2 cup chopped organic red onion
- Two tbsp. of red wine vinegar

**This is how you make it**:

Arrange all the ingredients in large bowl. Toss together.

Additionally you can complement this healthy salad with cherry tomatoes, peppers, dried cranberries, chopped cabbage, and slivered almonds, balsamic vinegar with extra virgin olive oil.

**Nutrition Information**:

Amount per Serving Calories 212 - fat 11 g - Saturated fat 4 g

Cholesterol 22 - Sodium 869 mg - Carbohydrate 20 g - fiber 6 g

Sugars 4 g - Protein 9 g

# 4. Delicious and Healthy Grilled Chicken Salad with Honey Citrus Dressing

Serves: 2

**Ingredients**:

- Two small chicken breasts, get rid of fat
- 3.5oz (100g) of organic lettuce
- 1/2 cup of organic cherry tomatoes
- 1 organic cucumber sliced
- 1/2 organic avocado, sliced

- 1/2 carrot finely sliced or grated
- 10 organic mandarin segments
- ½ cup of feta cheese
- Organic pepper for seasoning

Dressing Ingredients:

- Half cup of freshly squeezed organic orange Juice
- 1/4 cup freshly squeezed organic lemon Juice
- Two tbsp. of honey

**Recipe Method**:

1. Utilize cling wrap to place the chicken breast in between. Using a rolling pin or pound the chicken breast to make sure it gets cooked fast enough. Both sides of the chicken breast have to be sprayed using cooking spray. To cook you can use or griddle pan or a BBQ. Allow the chicken to rest once it is cooked by placing it on a platter covered with foil.

2. Arrange grated carrot, the lettuce, feta cheese, tomatoes halved and sliced organic cucumber onto a platter. Decorate with mandarin segments around the serving platter.

3. Wisk all the components in a large bowl to make the dressing.

4. Slice the chicken breast previously removing the foil and cut into four to five slices and then place those on top of your salad. Use cracked pepper to add some zing to your salad recipe.

5. Pour dressing over.

Nutritional Information:

Per serving - 564 Cal

Protein 77.6 g - Fat, total 13.1 g - Carbohydrate 28.5 g - sugars 4.6 g - Sodium 26 mg

# 5. Super Healthy Quinoa Salad

Serves: 8

**Ingredients**:

- 1/3 cup fresh organic lemon juice
- 1/3 cup of extra virgin olive oil
- 3 tablespoons of chopped fresh cilantro
- Sea salt and fresh ground black pepper, to taste
- 1 cup of rinsed and drained quinoa
- 1 tbsp. cumin seeds, toasted
- Sunflower oil to coat the grill
- Two cobs of fresh corn, remove husks and silk
- 1 cup of cooked black beans, drained
- 1 organic plum tomato, diced

- 1 organic zucchini or yellow zucchini squash, diced
- 1/4 cup finely chopped organic red onion
- Two organic avocados sliced

**Method**:

1. In a small bowl, whisk lemon juice, olive oil, cilantro, salt and pepper; set apart.

2. Bring two cups water to a boil using a saucepan; add cumin and quinoa. Now simmer until liquid is absorbed while covering and reducing heat to medium-low (12 minutes approx.) Let stand for 5 minutes after removing pan from the heat. Then uncover and fluff the quinoa with a fork and let cool for approximately ten minutes.

3. Use a grill and lightly oil with cooking oil. Put it on medium high temp. For approximately ten to 15 minutes grill corn until lightly charred and tender. (You can also boil cobs of corn in a large container of simmering water. Cover and cook for six to ten minutes until tender.) Wait until the corn cools, and then cut kernels from corn cob. (You can use a good corn stripper for this)

4. Mix the tomato, quinoa, zucchini, corn kernels, beans, avocado and onion in a large cooking container. Drizzle the lemon & cilantro dressing over top and toss to mix. Next refrigerate and cover the salad for approximately one hour to allow flavors to blend. (Or up to two days).

Nutrition Information:

 Per serving: Calories: 221, Total Fat: 11 g - Sat. Fat: 1.5 g

Monounsaturated Fat: 8 g - Polyunsaturated Fat: 2 g -
Carbs: 26 g

Fiber: 4.5 g - Sugars: 2 g - Protein: 6 g - Sodium: 23 mg -
Cholesterol: 0 mg

## 6. Delicious and Healthy Raspberry and Zucchini Salad

Serves: 4

Refreshing taste and colorful appearance, that is exactly what you find in this amazing mix of yummy raspberries and zucchini. Red raspberries are loaded with phytochemicals that contribute to your body detoxification and they also promote a healthy weight loss. This wonderful fruit contains essential dietary fiber that promotes your proper metabolic functions so you can burn those excess pounds faster. Eating raspberries in combination with zucchini promotes and regulates your normal bowel movements and proper digestive system functions in a natural and effective way. On top of these healthy powers, raspberries also help to regulate your blood sugar levels. So enjoy this light and clean recipe now!

**Ingredients**:

- Six large organic radishes, washed and finely sliced
- Two cups of washed and dried romaine lettuce leaves, torn into pieces
- Half cup of diced organic zucchini
- 1 1/2 cups fresh organic raspberries
- 6 tbsp. of extra-virgin olive oil
- Two tbsp. of freshly squeezed organic lemon juice
- 1 tbsp. of sea salt
- Two tbsp. of warm honey

**Method**:

1. In a medium bowl mix the lettuce, raspberries, radishes and zucchini. Set aside.
2. Whisk together the extra virgin olive oil in a smaller bowl. Add the organic lemon juice, sea salt, and honey until the dressing is properly mixed. Drizzle the dressing over the veggies and raspberries and softly toss. It is now ready to be served! Enjoy!

Approx. calories per serving: 390

## 7. Delicious Strawberry & Procsiutto Healthy Salad

Serves: 4 (serving size: 1 1/4 cups of salad and 1 tbsp. of dressing)

This is a very tasty salad that only takes about 10 minutes to prepare and just 5 minutes to cook and it is delicious. Enjoy!

**Ingredients**:

- 1 tbsp. of extra virgin olive oil
- Two tbsp. of balsamic vinegar
- 1 1/2 tbsp. honey
- 1/4 tbsp. of sea salt
- 1/2 tbsp. of freshly ground black pepper

- 1/3 cup sliced red organic onion
- 1 1/2 cups strawberries, sliced
- Olive oil cooking spray
- Four thin slices of prosciutto (approx. 2 oz.)
- 6 cups of organic baby arugula (approx. 5 oz.)
- Two ounces of feta cheese, crumbled (cheese can be used in a clean diet only if it is a low fat chees and in small quantities, you can use vegan parmesan cheese)

## Method:

1. In a large serving bowl whisk together extra virgin oil, balsamic vinegar, honey, sea salt and black pepper. Add red onion and berries; let it rest for 15 minutes approximately.

2. In the meantime, add a light layer of cooking spray over a cast-iron skillet or nonstick pan, and heat over moderately high heat. Cook prosciutto by adding a layer of it and turning sporadically for approx. five minutes or until it has a crispy consistency or brown gold. Move to a platter to cool; crumble and set aside.

3. Arrange the baby arugula in a big serving bowl with the feta cheese; add the red onion, the strawberries, and balsamic dressing, and lightly toss until just coated. Serve

the salad in 4 different salad bowls or plates, and then add the cooked prosciutto on top of each one.

Nutritional Information:

Calories per serving: 155 - Fat: 10g - Saturated fat: 4g

Monounsaturated: 3g - Polyunsaturated fat: 1g

Protein: 8g - Carbohydrates: 11g - Fiber: 2g

Cholesterol: 22mg - Iron: 1mg - Sodium: 534mg - Calcium: 105mg

## 8. Delicious and Refreshing Beetroot and Orange Salad

Orange gives this recipe very effective antioxidant powers to detox your body and get slim faster. Carotenoids contained inside this low calorie delicious fruit help to eliminate toxins from your system in a natural way. In fact a regular consumption of oranges can help to flush out unwanted toxins from your body and lose weight faster. With this special salad combination you get all the detox powers from oranges in a delicious and yummy way combined with other nutrients and vitamins found in beetroots. Beetroot is a superfood that also contributes to your body detox since it is full of vitamin C, magnesium and iron. Beetroot is also excellent for liver detox and to regulate cholesterol levels naturally. Arugula is a dark leafy green full of nutrients and also an essential component of most of the healthy salad recipes inside this book.

Serves 2

## Ingredients:

- Two cups of organic beetroots (sliced)
- 1 jar of all natural orange marmalade (no sugar)
- Three organic oranges
- One bunch of organic arugula

## Method:

1. Mix the arugula and sliced beetroots.

2. By mixing beetroots and the arugula dissolve the orange marmalade

3. Cut away the sides of the orange and cut out the segments.

4. Mix all the ingredients together – refrigerate in a large bowl until ready to serve.

This is a low calorie salad with approximately 300 calories per serving; you can also add some pecans to make it tastier. Enjoy!

## 9. Delicious and Healthy Tuna Salad with Egg

Serves: 3

**Ingredients**:

- One hard-cooked egg, chopped
- 3 oz. of light water tuna, drained and flaked
- 1/4 cup chopped organic celery
- 1/4 cup chopped sweet pickles
- 4 tbsp. of canola oil
- 2 tbsp. of mustard
- One organic cucumber sliced
- One bunch of organic romaine lettuce

**Method**:

Mix all of the components in a small bowl and combine them well. You can use this delicious mix as a yummy sandwich filling or serve with low sodium high fiber crackers.

---

Nutritional Information:

1 serving = 129 calories - 6 g fat (0 saturated fat) - 86 mg cholesterol

396 mg sodium - 7 g carbohydrate - fiber: 0 g – protein: 11 g.

---

# 10. Delicious and Healthy Quinoa and Tofu Salad

This amazing and delicious healthy salad is full of heart supporting components like vegetables, quinoa (whole grains) and legumes like soy-based tofu. Enjoy!

Serves: 6

Cooking Time: 25 minutes

Tot Time: 35 minutes

**Ingredients:**

- Two cups of pure water
- 1 cup quinoa, rinsed well

- 3/4 teaspoon of sea salt
- 1/4 cup of organic lemon juice
- 3 tbsp. of extra-virgin olive oil
- Two small cloves of organic garlic, minced
- 1/4 tbsp. of freshly ground pepper
- 8 oz. of baked smoked tofu, diced
- 1 small organic yellow bell pepper, diced
- 1 cup grape tomatoes, halved
- 1/2 cup chopped fresh organic mint
- 1 cup diced organic cucumber
- 1/2 cup chopped fresh organic parsley
- Feta cheese in cubes

**Method:**

1. Boil water with sea salt in a medium saucepan. Then after adding the quinoa let it boil again. Simmer until the water has been absorbed, for approximately 15 to 20 minutes. Cool the quinoa by spreading it on a baking sheet for about ten minutes.

2. Place the lemon juice, garlic, extra virgin olive oil, the remaining 1/4 tbsp. of sea salt and pepper in a large bowl while whisking all the ingredients. Add the cooled quinoa, cucumber, tofu, bell pepper, tomatoes, feta cheese, mint and parsley; toss well to mix.

Quinoa a very healthy protein-rich grain and it must be rinsed to remove the saponin, the quinoa´s natural covering.

Nutritional Information:

Per serving:  228 calories:  10 g fat – cholesterol 0 mg - carbohydrates 26 g -  protein 9 g – fiber 4 g -  sodium 376 mg -  potassium 418 mg

## 11.    Delicious and Healthy Zucchini and Corn Salad

**Ingredients**:

- 12 oz. of corn
- Three small organic zucchini, diced
- 3/4 large  sweet red pepper, diced
- 3/4 medium organic onion, chopped
- 3 oz. of chopped organic green chilies
- 1/2 cup of extra virgin olive oil
- 1/4 cup of fresh organic lime juice
- 1 1/2 tbsp. of cider vinegar
- 1/2 tbsp. of ground cumin
- 1 1/8 tbsp. of sea salt

- 3/8 tbsp. of garlic salt
- 3/4 tbsp. of black pepper

**Method**:

1. Toss corn, red pepper, zucchini, onion, red pepper and chilies in a large bowl.

2. Mix remaining ingredients in a jar with tight-fitting lid; shake well.

3. Drizzle over the salad and stir gently.

4. Let it cool and rest for some hours.

**Nutritional Information**:

Serving Size: 1 (213 g) - Servings Per Recipe: 6

Amount Per Serving: 298 Calories - Total Fat 19.2 g - Cholesterol 0.0

Sodium 449.8 mg - Total Carbohydrate 32.0 - Dietary Fiber 4.5 g

Sugars 4.0 Protein 5.2 g

## 12.    Delicious Cucumber & Avocado Salad

This is a very fast and easy salad recipe that you can enjoy anytime during the day to maintain a healthy slim figure and to satisfy your cravings. The avocado gives this super healthy salad a yummy creamy taste. Avocado contains powerful antioxidant substances such as lycopene and beta-carotene that when combined with other vegetables it increases the absorption of carotenoids in your body so you can detox and lose weight faster. You can also add organic tomatoes to this tasty salad so it is even more refreshing.

Serves: 4

**Ingredients**:

- 2 medium organic cucumbers, cubed
- two organic avocados, cubed
- 4 tbsp. chopped organic fresh cilantro
- 1 clove garlic, minced
- 2 tbsp. minced organic green onions (optional)
- 1/4 large lemon
- 1/4 tbsp. of sea salt
- black pepper to taste
- 1 organic lime
- One bunch of organic arugula
- Balsamic dressing

**Method**:

1. Combine cucumbers, arugula, cilantro and avocados, in a large bowl. Stir in sea salt, garlic, onions, and pepper. Pour lemon juice and lime juice over the top, and toss. Refrigerate and cover for about 30 minutes.

Nutrition Information:

Calories 186 kcal – Carbohydrates 15.5 g – Cholesterol 0 m – Fat 14.9 g

Fiber 8.3 g – Protein 3.1 g – Sodium 157 mg

# 13.    Delicious Shrimp & Feta Cheese Salad

## Ingredients:

- Three green organic onions, including tops
- 1/2 med.- size organic cucumber
- 1 lb. lg. shrimp
- 4 oz. pimento (1 jar)
- Two tbsp. snipped fresh dill or minced organic parsley
- 1 oz. rinsed and crumbled feta cheese (1/4 cup).

- Two tbsp. of organic lemon juice
- 2 tbsp. of extra virgin olive oil
- 1 tbsp. white wine vinegar
- 1 tsp. Dijon-style mustard or spicy brown mustard
- 1/2 tsp. black pepper
- 1 clove garlic, minced

**Method**:

1. Shell and devein shrimp. Slice onions thin. Peel, seed, and chop cucumber. Drain pimentos and pat dry.
2. Boil water. Add shrimp and cook, stirring until just firm, approx. for two minutes. Drain, rinse under cold running water, and drain over again.
3. Arrange shrimp in large bowl and add cucumber, green onions, pimentos, dill, and feta cheese. In small bowl whisk together lemon juice, garlic and pepper, olive oil, vinegar, and mustard. Drizzle over the shrimp mix and toss gently to combine.

## 14.    Super Healthy Chicken Caesar Salad

Serves: 4

**Ingredients:**

- 1 pound boneless, skinless chicken breasts, trimmed of fat
- 1 tbsp. of canola oil
- Freshly ground pepper, to taste
- 1/4 tbsp. of sea salt, or to taste
- 8 cups washed, dried and torn organic romaine lettuce
- 1 cup fat-free croutons
- 1/2 cup of light Caesar Salad Dressing
- 1/2 cup of low fat Parmesan Cheese grated

- Lemon wedges

**Method**:

1. Arrange a grill or preheat broiler.

2. Spray chicken with oil and season with salt and pepper. Grill or broil chicken until golden brown and no trace of pink remains in the center, approx. 3 to 4 minutes each side.

3. Using a large bowl mix croutons and romaine lettuce. Toss with Caesar Salad Dressing and divide among 4 plates. Cut chicken into 1/2-inch slices and fan over salad. Top with Parmesan curls. Serve immediately, with lemon wedges.

Nutrition Information:

Per serving: 278 calories - 6 g fat - cholesterol: 74 mg – carbohydrates 14 g protein 34 g – fiber: 1 g – sodium: 662 mg – potassium: 308 mg

# 15.    Delicious Corn & Avocado Salad

**Ingredients**:

- 1 sweet red pepper
- Three ears sweet corn
- One small organic red onion
- 3 Tablespoon of vegetables oil
- 1 Tablespoon of lime juice
- 1 Tablespoon red wine vinegar
- 1/2 tbs. salt
- 1/4 tbsp. of cayenne
- 1/4 tbsp. of freshly ground black pepper
- Two organic avocados
- 1 cup of organic cilantro leaves
- Four sliced radish
- Half a cup of sliced black olives

**Method:**

1. Put cut kernels from ears of corn in a large dish. Chop red onion and red pepper and add them to the corn kernels.

2. Mix oil, radish, vinegar, black olives, pepper, lime juice, salt and cayenne in a small bowl. Whisk to blend and transfer over corn mix. Carefully toss to coat your veggies.

3. Add pulverized cilantro leaves and to salad. Toss to mix. Now you can cover and refrigerate your salad for a few minutes and cool it prior to being served. When you are ready to serve your salad allow to come to room temp.

4. Add dice avocado prior to serving time and toss gently to mix.

# Healthy and Delicious Powerful Tips for Your Salad Recipes

Creating salads is more an art than anything else. Green salads are a great pillar of your clean eating diet and they can really be a main dish on their own or just a great side dish to accompany your healthy clean menus. These salads constitute a great snack to have any time of the day to satisfy your cravings with peace of mind knowing that you are not intoxicating your body with harmful processed foods. What makes the difference between a simple and a great salad can be just in the implementation of some helpful tips when you prepare them and when you choose the ingredients. Here is a list of some simple yet powerful tips that you can use to make your salads stand out:

- Make sure all the ingredients you are using are thoroughly washed unless you bought a pre-washed mix of veggies. Most of the times just washing your greens with water is not enough since some dirt and traces of pesticides may remain. So my advice is to use a product called citrus magic that is 100% natural and removes pesticides, chemicals, soil and waxes from your salad ingredients in a safely manner. Also you have to make sure that your veggies and fruits are dried prior of being mixed in a salad or else they will alter the dressing. You can us a salad spinner for this purpose and this is by the way one of the tools that you should have in your kitchen if you are serious about making salads.
- To turn your salads into a meal you can add protein ingredients like chicken, tuna, fish, salmon, egg whites, turkey breast. If you are 100% vegetarian you can add tofu, kidney beans, chickpeas and pinto beans. No fatty meats like bacon or salami should be part of your healthy clean salad recipes and no heavy sauces.
- You can add seeds and nuts to your healthy salad recipes to enhance flavor. Other ingredients you can add include anchovies and kalamatas.
- You can also roast some of your veggies on the grill before combining them into your healthy salads. Some ingredients like Portobello mushrooms,

asparagus, onions and zucchini taste really well when roasted.

- Toss your salads well and do not over dress them, just a small amount of dressing makes your salads yummy and tastier. Vinaigrette should be at the top of your list for dressings.
- Season your salads with sea salt and black pepper to make them sing!
- Use different types of vinegars and vegetable oils with your salads. There are different types of delicious vinegars to dress your salads like the orange muscat champagne vinegar with great flavor.
- Instead of vinaigrette you can also use lemon, orange, lime and even natural apple juice to dress your healthy salads.
- Some flavor enhancers like garlic, green onions, mustard and even honey work very well to spice up your recipes.
- Herbs like basil can also be combined with your salad recipes; you can try different herbs with your recipes and have fun experimenting and tasting them.
- Stay away from creamy dressings that only add more calories to your salad recipes.
- Incorporate a great variety of greens and veggies into your salads and don´t be afraid to combine them with some fruits so you can add that special touch to your recipes, be creative and enjoy the process of chopping, mixing and combining ingredients. Let

your salads be full of color and taste by adding carrots, red onions, broccoli, red peppers, green peppers, red peppers and an array of greens like parsley, arugula, chard, kale, radicchio, spinach and more... All this ingredients are full of nutrients and rich in antioxidants that will detox your body and make your digestive system to function better so you stay slimmer and stronger. Folic acid and lutein will enter your system through these healthy salad recipes so you can start feeling better from now on.

# 16.    Delicious Tuna Salad with Peppers and Beans

## Ingredients:

- 370 g (13 oz.) of tuna in spring water (flaked)
- 750g (26 oz.) four bean mix, drained, rinsed
- Four chopped organic tomatoes
- 1 small organic red onion, halved, thinly sliced
- Two large organic celery sticks, finely chopped
- One cup of flat-leaf parsley leaves, chopped

NOTE: you can try Recipe Convert App to convert recipe measurements

## Lemon dressing

- 1 large organic lemon, rind finely grated, juiced

- 1 organic garlic clove, crushed
- 1 tbsp. of extra-virgin olive oil
- 1/2 tbsp. of liquid stevia

**Method:**

1. In a large bowl place the flaked tuna. Add celery beans, tomato, parsley and onion.
2. Lemon dressing: mix lemon rind, 2 tbsp. of lemon juice, oil, garlic and stevia in a screw-top jar. Secure lid and shake until well combined.
3. Gently drizzle the dressing over salad. Spice it up with sea salt and pepper and stir to mix. Serve and enjoy!

# 17.  Delicious and Healthy Niçoise Salad

Serves: 6

**Ingredients**:

Vinaigrette

- 3/4 cup extra-virgin olive oil
- Half a cup lemon juice
- 1 medium shallot, minced
- 1 Tablespoon of minced fresh thyme leaves
- Two Tablespoon of minced fresh organic basil leaves
- Two tbsp. of minced fresh oregano leaves
- Sea Salt & freshly ground black pepper
- 1 tbsp. of Dijon mustard

## Salad

- Two cooked or otherwise grilled tuna steaks* (8 oz. each)
- Six hard-boiled eggs, peeled and either halved or quartered
- Ten small new red potatoes (each approx. two inches in diameter, about 1 1/4 pounds total), each potato scrubbed and quartered
- Sea Salt and freshly ground black pepper
- Two medium heads of organic butter lettuce or Boston lettuce, leaves washed, dried, and torn into bite-sized pieces
- Three small ripe tomatoes, cored and cut into eighths
- One small organic red onion, thinly sliced
- 8 oz. of green beans, stem ends trimmed and each bean halved crosswise
- 1/4 cup of niçoise olives
- 2 tablespoon of capers, rinsed (you can also use anchovies)

## Method:

*For about 1 hour marinate the tuna steaks in a little extra-virgin olive. Heat a large fry pan on medium high heat, or place on a hot grill. Cook the tuna steaks for about two to three minutes on each side until well cooked.

1. Whisk lemon juice, oil, shallot, thyme, basil, oregano, and mustard in medium bowl; season to taste with salt and pepper and set aside.

2. Boil red potatoes in a large pot. Add 1 tablespoon of sea salt and cook until potatoes are tender, approx. for five to eight minutes. Move potatoes to a medium bowl with a slotted spoon (don´t get rid of boiling water). Toss warm potatoes with 1/4 cup vinaigrette; set apart.

3. Toss lettuce with 1/4 cup vinaigrette in large bowl until coated while potatoes are cooking. Set a bed of lettuce on a serving dish. Slice tuna into half inch thick slices, covering with vinaigrette. Place tuna in the middle of lettuce. Toss red onion, tomatoes, 3 tbsp. of vinaigrette, and sea salt and pepper to taste in bowl; place tomato-onion mixture on the lettuce bed. Place the remaining potatoes in a mound at edge of lettuce bed.

4. Return water to boil; add 1 tbsp. of sea salt and green beans. Cook until it has a crisp & tender consistency, approx. three to five minutes. Drain beans, transfer to reserved ice water, and let rest till it gets cooler, approx. 30 seconds; then dry beans well. Toss beans, 3 tbsp. of

vinaigrette, and sea salt and pepper to taste; place in a mound at edge of lettuce bed.

5. Place hard boiled eggs, anchovies (if using) and olives, and in mounds on the lettuce bed. Shower eggs with remaining two tbsp. of dressing, sprinkle entire salad with capers (if using), and serve right away and enjoy!

## 18. Delicious & Healthy Tuna and Feta Cheese Salad

**Ingredients**:

- One can (3oz.) of White Tuna in Water
- 2 Cups shredded lettuce, mixed variety
- 4 Cherry tomatoes, halved
- ¼ of organic sliced cucumber
- Two Tablespoon feta cheese, crumbled
- Two Tablespoon of sliced black olives
- Two Tablespoon of Balsamic Vinaigrette

**Method**:

1. Drain tuna well.  Arrange salad greens on plate

2. Top with tuna, olives, tomatoes, cucumbers, and toss well.

Now sprinkle your salad with feta cheese. Drizzle with Balsamic Vinaigrette.

Nutrition Information:

Serving Size (392g)

Amount Per Serving: Calories300 - Calories from Fat 150 - Total Fat 17 g - Saturated Fat 3.5 g - Trans Fat   0 g – Cholesterol 55 mg - Sodium 840 mg

Total Carbohydrate 12 g - Sugars 7 g - Dietary Fiber 3 g

## 19.    Delicious and Healthy Strawberry and Spinach Salad

**Ingredients**:

Serves: 4

- Two tbsp. of sesame seeds
- 1 tbsp. of poppy seeds
- Half cup of extra-virgin olive oil
- 1 tbsp. of liquid stevia
- 1/4 cup distilled white vinegar
- 1/4 tbsp. of paprika
- 1/4 tbsp. of Worcestershire sauce
- 1 tbsp. of crushed onion
- Ten oz. of fresh organic spinach - rinsed, dried and torn into bite-size pieces

- 1/4 cup almonds, blanched and slivered
- 1 quart organic strawberries - cleaned, hulled and sliced

## Method:

1. Whisk together the sesame seeds, extra-virgin olive oil, paprika, poppy seeds, sugar, vinegar, Worcestershire sauce and onion in a medium bowl. Cover, and chill for about 1 hour.
2. Mix the spinach, strawberries and almonds in a large bowl. Then drizzle dressing over salad, and toss. Cool for about ten to 15 minutes prior to serving. Enjoy!

Nutrition Information:

Calories per serving: 490 – Fiber: 6.5 g – Carbohydrates: 43 g Cholesterol: 0

## 20.    Delicious & Healthy Spinach Tomato & Pineapple Salad

Serves: 4

**Ingredients**:

- Six cups of organic baby spinach leaves
- 1 1/2 cups of pineapple, cubed into bit sized pieces
- 1 1/2 cups cherry tomatoes, halved


Shallot Dressing:

**Method**:

Place the pineapple, spinach and tomatoes in a large bowl. Drizzle with some of the dressing, toss and serve.

Shallot Dressing Recipe:

Yield: 1 cup

- Half cup of shallots, diced
- 1/4 cup raw apple cider vinegar
- 2 tbsp. of date paste or 4 pitted dates
- 1 tbsp. of Dijon mustard
- 4-6 cloves roasted garlic (or to taste)
- 1/2 cup of pure water
- 2 tbsp. of fresh parsley
- Freshly ground pepper to taste

**Method**:

Mix all ingredients in a blender, blend until it has a smooth consistency. Enjoy!

## 21.    Delicious Cucumber & Broccoli Healthy Salad

Serves: 4

**Ingredients:**

- 1 medium organic cucumber
- Two small bunches of organic broccoli
- Half cup pine nuts
- 1/3 cup Feta cheese
- Two tbsp. of sliced green onion
- 1 tbsp. fresh Dill weed, minced
- 5 mint leaves, minced
- Sea Salt, fresh cracked pepper
- 1/3 cup plain Greek yogurt

- Half tbsp. of honey
- 1 tbsp. of light mayo
- 1 tbsp. fresh lime juice

**Method**:

1. Separate the broccoli florets from the stem and cut them into smaller pieces.
2. Cut the cucumber into straws.
3. Mix broccoli, mint, cucumber, Feta, dill weed, pine nuts, green onion, sea salt and pepper in a large mixing bowl. Stir until mixed together.
4. Mix Greek yogurt, honey, mayo, and lime juice in a small bowl.
5. Coat the veggies with the sauce until all veggies are uniformly covered.

Let it rest on the refrigerator for about two hours prior to serving and then stir one more time and enjoy!

## 22.   Delicious & Yummy Fruit Salad with Strawberries, Mango, Banana, Banana, Grapes, Peaches, Pineapple and Kiwi

Fruits have impressive and powerful detoxifying properties that can restore your digestive system and your regular bowel movements so you lose weight faster and in a healthy way. Strawberries are antioxidants rich like ellagic acid, a substance that effectively and naturally fights free radicals. On top of this strawberries are full of dietary fiber so you lose weight faster and easier. This amazing combination replenishes your body with all the nutrients it needs in a delicious and refreshing way.

**Ingredients:**

- 20 oz. of organic pineapple (tidbits drained)
- 20 oz. organic peaches
- One maraschino cherry (cut in half reserve juice)
- 2 orange peel (cut into chunks)
- 1 cup of organic blueberries
- Two cups of organic strawberries (quartered)
- 3 organic kiwi fruits (peeled and cut into chunks)
- Two organic mangoes (peeled and diced)
- One green organic apple (peeled and cut into chunks)
- Two organic bananas (firm, sliced thin)
- Two cups of organic grapes (white, halved)
- Two tbsp. of honey
- 2 cups grapes (black, halved)
- Two tbsp. cherry juice

**Method**:

1. Arrange all the fruit in a large bowl.
2. Depending upon how much juice you want in the salad, drizzle with honey on top of the fruit, 1/2 cup for more juice, 1/4 cup for less.
3. Add the cherry juice and stir to mix fruit and distribute the honey and cherry juice.
4. Place and cover in the fridge for approx.1 hour.
5. Prior to serving, thinly slice the banana and stir into the salad, mixing it with the juice.
6. Serve and enjoy!

Nutrition Information:

Amount Per Serving

Calories 336.9 - Calories from Fat 10 - Total Fat 1.1 g - Saturated Fat 0.2 g

Cholesterol 0.0 mg - Sodium 11.7 mg - Total Carbohydrate 87.3 g

Dietary Fiber 10.1 g - Sugars 67.8 g - Protein 3.9 g

## 23.    Fast & Easy Delicious Caprese Salad with Focaccia

Serves: 1

This is a very fast and easy meal to prepare. This makes a marvelous and healthy appetizer or snack anytime you are feeling hungry. Enjoy!

**Ingredients**:

- One cup halved cherry tomatoes (about 12)
- One oz. of sliced fresh mozzarella cheese
- 1 tbsp. chopped fresh basil
- 1 tbsp. balsamic vinegar
- 1 focaccia bread

**Method**:

Mix all the components together in a bowl, and serve with
the focaccia bread and enjoy!

Nutrition Information:

Per serving: 141 calories, 6.4g fat (3.5g saturated), 11.8g
carbohydrates, 2.5g fiber, 7.8g sugar, 9g protein

## 24.     Super-Fast & Easy Healthy Delicious Shrimp Salad

- 1 1/2 lbs. shrimp, cooked and deveined
- 1/4 cup extra virgin olive oil
- Organic lemon juice
- 1 clove of organic garlic, minced
- 1 tbsp. fresh parsley, chopped
- 1 organic cucumber sliced
- Sea salt and pepper, to taste

**Method**:

1. Cook, shell, and devein the shrimp. Mix remaining ingredients (excluding parsley) for the dressing.

2. Then drizzle the dressing over shrimp in a salad
   bowl, and mix until all ingredients are well coated.

Serve warm or cover and cool in the fridge for approx. one
hour. Sprinkle with fresh organic parsley before serving.
Enjoy!

This is a fast and easy yummy recipe with low calories that
you can enjoy as a meal or an appetizer any time during
the day.

# 25. Delicious and Healthy Mediterranean Quinoa Fresh Salad

Serves: 4 to 6

**Ingredients:**

- One cup of uncooked quinoa
- Two cups of pure water
- Half organic lemon squeezed
- 1/4 cup of organic red onion, diced
- 1/4 cup (about 10) kalamata olives, pitted and sliced
- Two tbsp. extra virgin olive oil
- Two cups of cucumber, peeled and diced (from 1 English)
- 1 cup cherry tomatoes, quartered
- Sea salt and fresh pepper, to taste
- 1/3 cup crumbled feta

**Method:**

1. Rinse quinoa for approx. two minutes, using your hands until you get rid of all the saponins.
2. Boil water in a medium size bowl, add quinoa and sea salt to taste. As soon as the H2O boils ease the heat to low and cover; simmer covered for fifteen minutes. Take away from the heat and while keeping it covered for another 5 minutes without lifting the lid; after that fluff with a fork and set apart in a large mixing bowl to cool.
3. Dice all the vegetables while the quinoa cool. Add the red onion, tomatoes, cucumber, olives, to the cooled quinoa, and squeeze half lemon over it.
4. Drizzle the olive oil over the quinoa, then add feta, sea salt and pepper to taste and toss well. Taste for salt and modify as needed, add more lemon juice if required.

# 26.    Super Easy & Healthy Organic Radish Salad

This is an excellent salad recipe to break down fats and detox. Radishes have diuretic powers that help to flush toxins outside of your system in a natural and effective way. The cilantro ingredient not only gives this salad a great taste but it also helps you to get rid of heavy metals and remove harmful toxins from your system. You can practically use this super healthy herb in many if not all of your healthy clean recipes to get all the detox benefits it has.

Serves: 4 to 6

**Ingredients**:

- Two tbsp. of apple cider
- Two tbsp. of extra virgin olive oil
- Two tbsp. orange juice
- Two tbsp. fresh lime juice
- 1 tbsp. of honey
- Sea salt and freshly ground black pepper
- 12 oz. of organic radishes, trimmed and each cut into wedges
- 1/4 cup finely chopped organic red onion
- 1/4 cup fresh organic cilantro leaves

**Method**:

Whisk together the cider, extra virgin-olive oil, orange juice, lime juice, and honey until the honey dissolves in a large bowl. Then taste and spice it up with a pinch of sea salt and pepper. Add the radish wedges, red onion and cilantro. Toss gently and cool in the fridge for approx. 1 hour. You can enjoy this super healthy salad at room temperature of cold.

## 27.     Refreshing & Delicious Vegetarian Salad With Tomatoes & Cucumber

This is a wonderful and very refreshing salad full of nutrients and antioxidants. This salad is great for a fat burning and colon cleansing diet, you can add some type of protein if you want transform it into a full meal. Egg whites, chicken or salmon will work just fine. Enjoy! To detox I suggest this healthy salad as a great start to prepare your body for a full green juice detox.

Serves: 6

**Ingredients**:

- 1/3 cup red wine vinegar
- 1 tbsp. of liquid stevia
- Two large organic cucumbers, peeled, seeded, and sliced into half inch slices
- 1 tbsp. of sea salt
- Three large organic tomatoes, seeded and chopped
- 2/3 cup chopped red onion
- 1/2 cup chopped fresh mint
- 2 tbsp. of extra virgin olive oil
- Sea salt and pepper to taste

**Method**:

1. Mix vinegar, stevia, and sea salt in a large bowl. Add sliced cucumbers, and marinate for approx. one hour, stirring occasionally.
2. Gently toss tomatoes, mint, onion, and olive oil with the marinated organic cucumbers. Spice it up with sea salt and pepper.

---

Nutrition Information:

Calories: 89 – Fiber: 1.8 g – Carbohydrates: 11.5 g – Cholesterol: 0 mg

Protein: 1.6 g – Fat: 4.7 g – Sodium 559 mg

Salads

# 28.    Delicious Vegetarian Salad with Avocado Cherry Tomatoes and Corn

**Ingredients**:

For Salad:

- 1 cup chopped organic tomatoes or cherry/grape tomatoes
- Three cups spring mix salad
- 1 large organic avocado, chopped into bite-sized chunks
- 1/2 cup corn kernels (fresh corn recommended, not frozen)
- 8 oz. (about 1 cup) fresh mozzarella, cut into bite-sized chunks

- Half cup fresh basil

For Vinaigrette:

- Juice from 1 lemon
- 2 Tbsp. balsamic vinegar
- 1/4 cup olive oil
- Salt and pepper, to taste

**Method**:

1. Mix all ingredients for salad in a large bowl. Toss to evenly distribute.
2. Combine balsamic vinegar and lemon juice in a small bowl, while constantly whisking, add olive oil. Season with salt and pepper.
3. Pour vinaigrette over salad before serving; give it a gentle toss, and place on serving plates.

Enjoy!

This healthy and delicious salad can be transformed into a full meal with protein by adding fish, tuna or chicken.

Tip: You can even use the avocados as your serving plates! It looks perfect and deliciously super **healthy YUMMY**! This is a great idea if you want to surprise your guests at the table.

## 29.    Healthy & Delicious Quinoa and Black Beans Salad

You can prepare and move forward with the other components of this super **healthy YUMMY** salad while you wait for the quinoa to cook.

Serves: 4 to 6

**Ingredients**:

- 1 cup uncooked organic grain quinoa, well rinsed
- 1/2 tbsp. of sea salt
- Two cups of pure water
- Two tbsp. of lime juice
- 1/3 cup diced organic red onion
- 1 15-ounce can black beans, drained and rinsed

- 1 cup frozen corn, defrosted, OR 1 cup of fresh corn, parboiled, drained and cooled (approximately the amount of kernels from one ear of corn)
- Three medium tomatoes, seeded and cut into chunks
- 5 oz. of feta cheese cut into 1/4-inch to 1/2-inch cubes
- 1 jalapeño, seeded and finely chopped (optional)
- Three tbsp. of extra virgin olive oil
- 1/4 cup chopped cilantro, including tender stems, packed

**Directions:**

1. Put the rinsed quinoa, sea salt and water into a pot and bring it to a boil. Cover and simmer gently until the quinoa absorbs all the water, approx. for ten to fifteen minutes. Remove from heat and let it rest for five minutes approx. Arrange into a large container and fluff up with a fork to help it cool faster.

2. Prepare the rest of the salad while the quinoa is cooking. Soak the red onions in the lime juice and set apart. Soaking the onions in lime juice (or lemon juice or water) helps take the edge off of them. In a large bowl combine corn kernels, the prepped black beans, tomatoes, feta cheese, jalapenos, cilantro, and oil into a large bowl.

3. Once the quinoa has cooled, combine it into the bean mix. Add the lime juice and red onion and add sea salt, extra oil or lime juice to taste. Serve at room temp.

Note: you can also try to make this healthy salad by combining the quinoa with dried cranberries and slivered almonds so you get a delicious blend too. To replace the cheese you can also sprinkle this salad recipe with some raw pumpkin seeds instead. Enjoy!

Salads

## 30.    Healthy and Delicious Watermelon Salad

This is an amazingly delicious refreshing salad that can be enjoyed as a super healthy snack anytime during the day. You can also use fresh mint instead of cilantro for this super healthy recipe.

**Ingredients**:

- Three tablespoons lime juice
- 1 cup sliced red onion, cut lengthwise
- 15 cups cubed watermelon
- 3 cups cubed English cucumber
- 1 (8 ounce) package feta cheese, crumbled
- 1/2 cup chopped fresh cilantro

- sea salt
- cracked black pepper

**Method:**

1. Drizzle lime juice over red onions in a small bowl. Allow to marinate while preparing the salad.
2. Gently mix the watermelon, feta cheese, cucumber, and cilantro in a large bowl. Spice it up with black pepper. Toss watermelon salad with marinated onions and season with sea salt just prior to serving.

Nutrition Information:

Calories: 94 kcal – Carbohydrates: 14.2 g – Cholesterol: 13 mg – Fat: 3.5 g

Fiber: 1 g – Protein: 3.4 g

# 31.     Super Healthy Cabbage Green Salad

A great tip to maintain this salad crisp is to soak your veggies in iced water and after that you can use a salad spinner to drain the water and prior to tossing them with the dressing.

**Ingredients**:

- 1 1/4 pounds Savoy cabbage, very thinly sliced on a mandoline (6 cups)
- 1 medium sweet onion, very thinly sliced on a mandolin

- 1 1/2 pounds fennel bulbs—halved, cored and very thinly shaved on a mandolin
- Iced water
- 1 seedless cucumber, halved lengthwise and sliced crosswise 1/8 inch thick
- Sea salt
- 1 cup crème fraîche
- Two tbsp. white wine vinegar
- 1/2 cup chopped dill
- Three tbsp. of poppy seeds

**Method**:

1. Arrange the cabbage, onion and fennel in three separate bowls and cover with ice water; let it rest for approx. 30 minutes. Drain the vegetables and spin dry in a salad spinner. In another bowl, toss the cucumbers with two tbsp. of sea salt and cover with ice water. Let it rest for 30 minutes, then drain and pat dry.
2. Whisk the crème fraîche with the vinegar in a large bowl, until stiff. Add the dill and poppy seeds and spice it up with sea salt. Fold in the fennel, cabbage, cucumber and onion, and serve right away. Enjoy!

# 32. Delicious Italian Bread Salad or Panzanella

This super yummy salad is made with the leftovers of bread. The use of stale bread makes this salad unique since the bread absorbs all the dressing flavors and stays deliciously crunchy ate the same time. In the traditional Italian cuisine nothing is wasted.

**Ingredients:**

- 1 day-old ciabatta loaf, crusts cut off, cut into cubes
- 1 oz. of extra-virgin olive oil
- 3 oz. of balsamic vinegar
- One organic garlic clove, crushed
- 5 organic ripe tomatoes, roughly chopped
- One small red onion, finely sliced
- Half a bunch of organic basil
- Sea Salt and pepper

**Method**:

1. In a preheated oven bake the bread until golden brown and dry. Let it cool.

Toss the bread with vinegar and the extra virgin olive oil in a bowl. Add the organic tomato and the organic onion and tear in the basil leaves. Toss again, spice it up to taste and now it is ready to be served and enjoyed!

This is a low calorie salad.

## 33.    Delicious Mediterranean Salad with Cherry Tomatoes and Mozzarella

This easy and refreshing salad is made with small balls of mozzarella cheese and cherry tomatoes. In a clean diet you have to limit the amount of saturated fat you eat, therefore eating small amounts of cheese is alright. Opt for a reduced fat mozzarella cheese.

**Ingredients**:

- Four cups (1 1/4 lb.) of cherry tomatoes rinsed and stemmed
- 8 oz. small balls fresh low fat mozzarella cheese
- 1/2 cup loosely packed fresh basil leaves, rinsed
- 2 tbsp. of extra-virgin olive oil

- Sea salt
- Black Pepper

**Method**:

   With a sharp knife cut the cherry tomatoes in 1/2. Tear basil leaves into tiny pieces. Combine cherry tomatoes, basil and mozzarella in a medium size bowl. Drizzle with 2 tbsp. of extra virgin olive oil and sprinkle lightly with sea salt and pepper; add more oil and sea salt to taste.

Nutrition Information

Per serving: Calories: 140 - Protein: 6.9g - Fat: 11g - Saturated fat: 5g

Carbohydrate: 4.3g - Fiber: 1.4g - Sodium: 123mg - Cholesterol: 25mg

## 34.    Delicious Carrots and Cucumber Salad

Serves: 2

**Ingredients**:

- 1/4 cup seasoned rice vinegar
- One tbsp. of liquid stevia
- 1/2 tbsp. vegetable oil
- 1/4 tbsp. grated peeled ginger
- 1/4 tbsp. of sea salt
- One cup of sliced carrot
- 2 tbsp. of sliced green onion
- Half organic cucumber - halved lengthwise, seeded, and sliced

- 2 tbsp. minced red bell pepper

**Method**:

1. Whisk rice vinegar, sugar, vegetable oil, ginger, and salt together in a bowl until sugar and salt are dissolved into a smooth dressing.
2. Toss carrot, green onion, bell pepper, and cucumber in the dressing to evenly coat.
3. Cover bowl with plastic wrap and refrigerate until chilled, about 30 minutes.

Nutrition Information

Calories 59 kcal Carbohydrates 11.5 g – Cholesterol 0 mg – Fat 1.4 g

Fiber 2.4 g – Protein 1.2 g – Sodium 336 mg

### 35. Delicious Penne Pasta Salad with Salmon and Broccoli

## Ingredients:

- 1 lb of whole grain penne pasta
- Sea salt
- fresh ground black pepper
- 8 oz. of smoked salmon, cut into 1 inch pieces
- 1/2 lb frozen green pea
- 1 cup of organic broccoli
- 1 lemon
- 1/2 organic lemon juice
- 2 tbsp. of extra virgin olive oil
- ½ cup of green onions
- 1 cup chicken stock

- fresh dill (to garnish)

**Method**:

1. In salted boil water cook the pasta.
2. Cook, stirring until the pasta is "al dente".
3. Drain the pasta and return it to the warm pot.
4. Add the peas, smoked salmon, lemon zest, lemon juice, broccoli, olive oil, green onions, and stock.
5. Simmer till heated through.
6. Stir.
7. Add sea salt and pepper to taste.
8. Garnish with fresh dill.

Nutrition Information:

Calories 597.5 - Calories from Fat 109 - Total Fat 12.1 g - Saturated Fat 3.4 g

Cholesterol 23.2 mg - Sodium 644.5 mg - Total Carbohydrate 100.3 g

Dietary Fiber 14.8 g - Sugars 4.1 g - Protein 23.9 g

Salads

## 36.  Delicious & Healthy Tofu, Tomatoes and Arugula Salad

This yummy salad can be served as a complete meal and it is very easy to prepare and also super healthy. The tofu ingredient gives this marvelous easy recipe more nutritional power and protein while soaking flavor from green onions and tomatoes. You can sprinkle some feta cheese to enhance this salad recipe and some sea salt.

Serves: 4

**Ingredients**:

- 1 (12-oz.) package extra firm tofu, drained
- 2 tbsp. of extra virgin olive oil

- Two Cloves of garlic, minced
- 1 bunch green onions, cut into 1/4-inch long pieces
- 4 small organic tomatoes, cut into 1/4-inch pieces
- 2 tbsp. fresh basil, chopped, or 1 teaspoon dried basil leaves
- 1/4 cup crumbled feta cheese
- Sea salt
- freshly ground black pepper

**Method:**

1. Cut block of tofu in 1/2 and lay on paper towels. Cover top with kitchen paper towels and press down to remove some of the fluid. Cut into half inch square pieces.

2. Heat the extra olive oil in a big sauté pan over medium high heat. Add tofu and sauté until golden brown on all sides, approx. 10 minutes. Add garlic and heat for two minutes. Add organic green onions and cook for two minutes. Take away from heat and stir in tomato and basil. Distribute between four serving platters and garnish with crumbled feta cheese. Enjoy!

## 37.     Delicious & Refreshing Cucumber and Apple Salad

This is a very refreshing and healthy salad recipe for a hot day or just to be enjoyed as a low calorie snack anytime during your day. Its mild sweet natural flavor makes this recipe a must try in your healthy clean eating menus. Enjoy!

Serves: 1-2

**Ingredients**:

- One organic cucumber, peeled
- One medium sweet organic red apple
- One tbsp. of honey

- One tbsp. of lemon juice
- One tbsp. of apple cider vinegar
- sprinkle some sesame seeds

**Method**:

Combine together lemon juice, honey, apple cider vinegar, and sesame seeds. Cut the organic cucumber into thin slices, and apple into bite size chunks or slices. Stir into dressing mixture. This super healthy recipe serves one big plate or two small bowls of salad.

Nutrition Information

Amount Per Serving: Calories: 166.7 - Total Fat: 0.8 g - Cholesterol: 0.0 mg

Sodium: 5.9 mg - Total Carbs: 42.8 g - Fiber: 4.9 g - Protein: 1.4 g

## 38. Delicious Pasta Salad with Mozzarella and Tomatoes

Serves: 8

**Ingredients**:

Dressing:

- 6 tbsp. of extra-virgin olive oil
- Half cup of sun-dried tomato packed in oil, drained
- 1/4 cup red wine vinegar
- 1 tbsp. capers, drained
- 1 garlic clove, minced

Salad

- 1 lb. medium pasta shell (use gluten free organic pasta)

- 2 cups cherry tomatoes, halved
- 8 ounces water-packed fresh mozzarella cheese, drained and cut into 1/2 inch pieces
- Half cup chopped kalamata olive
- 1 cup fresh basil leaf, thinly sliced
- 1/2 cup freshly grated low fat parmesan cheese

**Method**:

1. Boils water in a large pot.
2. Meanwhile, in a food processor, make dressing: combine all dressing ingredients.
3. Process until sun dried tomatoes are coarsely chopped.
4. Transfer to small bowl and set aside.
5. Add one teaspoon of salt and pasta to boiling water, stirring occasionally to prevent sticking.
6. Cook until pasta is tender (about 11 min.) and drain well.
7. Transfer to a large serving bowl.
8. Add dressing to hot pasta and toss to coat.
9. Let cool, stirring occasionally.
10. Add tomatoes, mozzarella, basil, Parmesan, and olives.
11. Spice it up to taste with sea salt and pepper.
12. Toss to mix and serve at room temperature.

## Nutrition Information

Calories per serving 440 - Calories from Fat 180 - Total Fat 20g

Cholesterol 25mg  - Sodium 440mg - Potassium 380mg
    11%

Total Carbohydrate 48g - Dietary Fiber 3g - Sugars 5g - Protein 17g

## 39.     Super Healthy & Delicious Asparagus and Radicchio Salad

Serves: 8

**Ingredients**:

- ¼ cup of extra-virgin olive oil
- ½ cup pine nuts
- 1 bunch asparagus, trimmed and cut on an angle into two inch sections
- Sea Salt and pepper
- 1 head of organic radicchio, quartered lengthwise and finely sliced crosswise
- 1 pound of Belgian endive (about 3 heads), halved lengthwise and thinly sliced crosswise

- 1 tbsp. of chopped pepperoncini
- Two cloves of organic garlic, thinly sliced
- 3 tbsp. of balsamic vinegar
- ¼ cup of chopped fresh organic parsley

**Method**:

1. Heat one and a half tbsp. of extra-virgin olive oil on medium heat in a medium nonstick skillet. Add the pine nuts and fry, stirring occasionally, until golden, about 5 minutes; move to a plate.
2. In the same skillet, heat one and a half tbsp. of extra virgin olive oil over medium heat. Add the asparagus and cook until it has a bright green and crisp-tender consistency, approx. for approx. two minutes; add some sizzle with salt and pepper. Transfer to a large bowl and toss with the radicchio, endive and pepperoncini.
3. In the same skillet, heat the remaining 3 tablespoons olive oil over medium heat. Supplement with garlic and cook for about one minute. Stir in the vinegar and spice it up with sea salt and pepper. Cook until slightly reduced, about two minutes. Drizzle over the salad, add the pine nuts and parsley and toss to coat.

# 40. Delicious & Healthy Hearts of Palm Avocado and Tomato Salad

Serves: 4

**Ingredients**:

- 15 oz. of hearts of palm (1/2 of a 25 oz. jar), drained and cut into slices
- Two small organic avocados, diced
- Two tbsp. of fresh squeezed organic lime juice
- One cup of small grape tomatoes, cut in 1/2
- 1/4 cup thinly sliced green organic onion (you can also use cilantro)
- 1/2 cup chopped cilantro (if desired)
- Mediterranean sea salt to season

**Method**:

1. Place palm hearts into a colander located in the sink and let them drain while you prepare the other ingredients. Dice avocados, put them in big bowl so you can put all the salad components, and toss with two tbsp. of fresh organic lime juice.

2. Cut the hearts of palm into small rings (or slice them in ½ if they don't cut easily.) Slice the grape tomatoes into 1/2. Cut the green organic onions and chop the cilantro (if you are using cilantro).

3. Toss the tomatoes, hearts of palm and green onions with the avocado and the lime juice blend, and then add extra lime juice to taste. Use the Mediterranean Sea Salt to season this yummy salad to taste and use chopped cilantro (if using) to add to the mix.

You can serve this salad immediately or store it in your freezer for a few hours and then it will be ready. Enjoy this low calorie salad now!

## 41.    Delicious & Refreshing Pineapple and Avocado Salad

Serves: 12

This salad is perfect to be enjoyed as a refreshing appetizer anytime during the day; it is booth healthy and refreshing!

**Ingredients**:

- One and a half cups of organic cucumbers - peeled, seeded, and cubed
- Half cup chopped red organic onion
- 1 cup of sun-maid seedless raisins

- Two tbsp. of lime juice
- 3/4 teaspoon of sea salt
- 2 1/2 cups of organic pineapple, peeled and cut into half inch dice
- Two organic avocados - peeled, pitted and diced

**Method**:

1. Mix the onion, cucumbers, seedless raisins, lime juice, and sea salt in a big bowl. Add the avocado and pineapple. Lightly toss to combine.

Nutrition Information

Calories 77 kcal – Carbohydrates 8.7 g – Cholesterol 0 mg – Fat 5 g

Fiber 3 g Protein 1.1 g – Sodium 149 mg

## 42.     Delicious & Healthy Arugula, Beetroot and Pineapple Salad

This delicious salad is not only great for losing weight and detox but it also has anti-inflammatory powers thanks to the pineapple ingredient that contains an antioxidant called bromelain. Enjoy!

Serves: 4

**Ingredients**:

- Four cups torn arugula leaves
- 1/4 fresh organic pineapple - peeled, cored, and chopped
- 1/4 red organic onion, finely sliced

- 1/4 cup chopped fresh organic cilantro
- Three tbsp. of apple cider vinegar
- 1 tbsp. of extra virgin olive oil
- Two tbsp. of honey
- 1/4 tbsp. of Sea Salt

**Method**:

1. Combine red onion, arugula, pineapple, and cilantro in a salad bowl. Whisk extra virgin olive oil, apple cider vinegar, honey, and sea salt in a small bowl; drizzle dressing over salad and toss to coat.

Nutrition Information

Calories 64 kcal – Carbohydrates 7.7 g - Cholesterol 0 mg – Fat 3.6 g

Fiber 0.9 g Protein 0.8 g – Sodium 154 mg

## 43.    Delicious Thai Style & Cucumber Salad

This makes a perfect side dish or even a wonderful light meal that you can incorporate to your healthy clean eating menus.

Serves: 2

**Ingredients**:

- 1/4 cup of Pat Thai sauce *
- One tablespoon of fresh cilantro (chopped)
- One tablespoon of peanuts (chopped) or you can use walnuts instead
- One tablespoon of rice vinegar
- Two tablespoon of liquid stevia
- One tablespoon of fish sauce

- 35 tablespoon of red pepper flakes
- one tablespoon of toasted Asian sesame oil
- One organic cucumber (finely sliced)
- 35 tablespoon of ginger root (minced fresh)

**Method**:

Whisk together the Thai sauce, peanuts, cilantro, rice vinegar, stevia, sesame oil, fish sauce, red pepper flakes, and ginger in a big bowl. Stir in the cucumber. Cover and cool down for ten minutes before serving.

*Note: to replace the Pat Thai sauce you can use tomato-paste mixture with 2 tbsp. of lime juice that will result in a version of this Asian classic with its sweet-and-sour balance.

Nutrition Information

Calories 113 kcal - Carbohydrates 17.6 g – Cholesterol 0 mg – Fat 4.8 g

Fiber 1.6 g – Protein 2.1 g – Sodium 223 mg

## 44.     Delicious Sesame Chicken Salad

Serves: 4

**Ingredients**:

- 3/4 cup of light maple syrup
- 1/3 cup Tamari soy sauce
- 1/2 cup sweet hot mustard
- 1/2 cup sesame seeds, a mix of black and white or all white
- 1/4 cup vegetable oil, 3 or 4 turns of the pan, total
- 1 1/3 pounds chicken breast tenders
- Sea Salt and black pepper

Salad Dressing:

- One and half inches of fresh ginger root, grated or minced
- three tbsp. of rice vinegar
- 1/4 cup Chinese duck sauce
- 1/4 cup vegetable oil

Salad:

- 5 to 6 ounces mixed baby greens, 1 bag
- 1 /4 English or seedless cucumber, halved lengthwise then thinly sliced on an angle
- 1 /2 cup shredded carrots, a couple of handfuls
- 4 scallions, finely sliced on an angle
- 1/4 pound snow peas, sliced on an angle
- Fried Chinese noodles for garnish

**Method**:

1. Mix syrup, soy and sweet hot mustard in a bowl. Season chicken tenders with sea salt and black pepper equally on both sides. Add chicken tenders to half of the marinade and coat. Set apart. Save the residual half for dressing.
2. Preheat a large nonstick skillet over medium high heat. Using a plate extent the sesame seeds. Dip the chicken tenders into the sesame seeds. Cover the cooking pan with a thin layer of oil. Cook chicken in

small batches three minutes on each side and move to plate.

3. Whisk ginger, vinegar and the reserved marinade together then stream in the oil while you continue to whisk the dressing.

4. Mix all of the salad ingredients in a bowl. Top your salad with the sesame chicken tenders and toss with dressing and serve. Add some crunch to your salad with fried noodles and enjoy!

*Salads*

## 45.    Delicious & Healthy Quinoa Salad with Peppers and Tomatoes

I use lime juice to cook the quinoa for this delicious salad recipe so it gets a mild citrus flavor and enhances its detox powers. In fact lime juice is excellent to detox your system and one marvelous trick that I want to share with you is that a very effective way to cleanse and purify your digestive system is by drinking every morning a glass of warm water with lime juice. You will be amazed with the great results you get with this simple and healthy technic that detoxifies your body and helps you stay slim.

**Ingredients:**

- 1/2 cup of extra-virgin olive oil
- Two cups of quinoa, rinsed and drained
- Two cups of fresh lime juice
- Two cups of pure water
- Sea Salt
- One large yellow pepper
- One large red bell pepper
- Half cup of pine nuts
- 1 tbsp. of white wine vinegar
- 1 ½ organic cucumber (sliced)
- 1 large organic beef tomato, seeded and finely diced
- Ground black pepper
- 1/4 cup of thinly chopped basil
- 1/4 cup thinly chopped mint

**Method:**

1. Use a saucepan to heat the extra virgin olive oil. Cook the quinoa in the saucepan over moderately high heat while stirring, until lightly browned, for approx. four minutes. Add the lemon juice, pure water and a substantial

amount of sea salt and bring to a boil. Cook on low heat for 15 minutes while the lemon juice is absorbed by the quinoa and that grain becomes translucent. Move the quinoa with a fork and extent on a baking sheet until it cools.

2. In the meantime, roast the yellow and red peppers directly over a broiler or a gas flame, turning sporadically, until it is well-cooked. Move the peppers to a bowl and then cover and let steam for ten minutes. Peel and seed the peppers and slice them into ¼ inch dice.

3. Toast the pine nuts over moderate heat using a medium skillet, stir sporadically, until golden and fragrant, approx. for five minutes. Move the pine nuts to a platter to cool.

4. Whisk the remaining 1/4 cup of extra virgin olive oil with the vinegar in a large bowl. Add the pine nuts, the quinoa, peppers, tomato, cucumber, mint and basil and toss well, make sure to break up any lumps of quinoa. With sea salt and the ground black pepper spice up this yummy and healthy salad.

Nutrition Information:

Calories per serving: 232 cal - 28 g carb - 11 g fat - 3 g of fiber

1.5 g sat fat - 7 g protein

## 46.    Easy & Delicious Avocado and Shrimp Salad

Serves: 4

**Ingredients:**

- 1/4 cup of extra virgin olive oil
- 1/4 cup of white wine vinegar
- One green organic onion, finely sliced
- 1/2 lb of small shrimp, cooked, de-veined and peeled
- Two ripe organic avocados
- Butter Lettuce
- Two Tbsp. of chopped roasted walnuts or pistachios
- One Tbsp. of chopped cilantro
- Organic lemon slices for garnish

**Directions**:

1. Mix green organic onions, oil, vinegar, and in a bowl. Chop shrimp into half inch pieces and add to oil mix.

2. Place leaves of lettuce on individual dishes. Cut avocados in 1/2 and get rid of pits. Get rid of some of the avocado around the pit area and combine with the shrimp. Using an avocado slicer or a spoon, gently scoop out avocado halves from their skins in one piece. Place avocado half on plate with lettuce. (An avocado slicer is a must have tool if you are serious about your love for salads)

3. Spoon shrimp mixture on to avocado. Sprinkle with cilantro and walnuts. Enjoy!

Serve with lemon slices for garnish and add some lemon juice drops and sea salt to season this marvelous healthy recipe, it is just SUPER YUMMY!

## 47.    Delicious & Healthy Spring Mix Salad with Feta Cheese

Serves: 6

**Ingredients**:

- 1 package (10 oz.) of mixed salad greens
- One ripe organic avocado - peeled, pitted and chopped
- 1 ripe organic tomato, chopped
- oz. of black olives, drained
- Six Greek pepperoncini peppers
- 1/4 cup of extra virgin olive oil
- 1 tbsp. of dried basil
- Two tbsp. of white vinegar
- Two tbsp. of garlic salt

- 1 tbsp. of dried organic oregano
- 5 oz. of feta cheese

**Method**:

1. In a large bowl, toss together the mixed greens, olives, tomato, avocado and pepperoncini peppers. Set apart.

2. Whisk together the oil, garlic salt, vinegar, oregano and basil in a small bowl. Pour over the salad mix and toss to coat. Sprinkle with feta cheese and enjoy!

## 48. Delicious Arugula, Avocado and Watermelon Salad

This is a lovely and refreshing delish salad excellent to detox your system and to lose weight while preserving your health with rich antioxidants and nutrients.

**Ingredients**:

- Five ounces of organic arugula, washed and spun dry
- Two cups of cubed seedless organic watermelon
- One organic avocado, cubed

- 1/8 cup extra virgin olive oil
- Organic lime juice
- Sea Salt and freshly ground pepper
- 1/4 tbsp. of cayenne pepper

**Method**:

1. Toss the arugula and watermelon in a large salad bowl. Set separately.

2. Whisk together the extra virgin olive oil, cayenne pepper, lime juice, and sea salt and pepper to taste in a medium bowl. Add cubed avocado to the vinaigrette and toss softly. This is an important step to stop the avocado from browning in the mix.

3. Now you can add avocado and vinaigrette to the salad container and gently toss to mix. Use fresh ground black pepper to season your salad and enjoy!

# 49. Refreshing Pomegranate and Pink Grapefruit Salad

Serves: 2

**Ingredients**:

- 1 tbsp  shallot (finely chopped)
- 1 tbsp  fresh lime juice
- 1 1/2 tbsps  olive oil
- 1/4 tsp  honey
- 1/4 tsp  salt
- 1  grapefruit (pink or red)
- 1/4 lb  mustard greens (young, trimmed and cut into 1/2 inch pieces 2 cups)
- 1/4 cup  dried date (pitted and chopped)

- pomegranate seeds

**Method**:

1. Stir together shallot and lime juice in a small bowl and let stand 5 minutes. Whisk in oil, honey, and salt.
2. Cut peel and any white pith from grapefruit with a sharp knife, and then cut sections free from membranes. Toss mustard greens with dates in a large bowl.
3. Just before serving, toss greens with dressing and salt to taste. Divide salad between 2 plates and top with grapefruit sections.

# 50.     Delicious Couscous and Pomegranate Salad

Serves 2

**Ingredients:**

- 1 cup  of couscous
- boiling water
- 1 tbsp. of extra virgin olive oil
- 2 tsps.  sherry wine vinegar
- 1/2 tsps. Mediterranean Sea Salt
- 1 tsp.  of lemon juice
- 1 cup of diced dried apricot
- 2 1/2 cups of pomegranate seeds
- 1  diced organic green pepper
- 1 cup of organic cauliflower

**Method**:

1. Arrange the couscous in a big mixing dish. Add extra virgin olive oil, cauliflower, and vinegar, Mediterranean Sea Salt and lemon juice. Stir.

2. Pour boiling water over the couscous until just covered. Stir. Add more pure water if you notice that the couscous is still dry. Cover dish and let it rest for approx. six mins.

3. With a fork fluff the couscous. Depending on the couscous consistency, add more pure water, cover and let sit another few minutes.

4. Add pomegranate seeds and green pepper.


Prep Time: 10 minutes

Cook Time: 10 minutes, tot time: 20 mins.

## Conclusion:

I want to thank you for reading this book and I hope you enjoy all the recipes. My goal is to help you have a better and healthier way of eating while you enjoy preparing these clean salad recipes.

Clean eating has many health benefits such as better sleep habits, increased energy and weight loss. I hope this healthy diet will help you get started with your clean eating lifestyle. Always take care of your body and have a healthy lifestyle, **I wish you a healthy and happy life!**

# Other Book Titles You May Like

http://tinyurl.com/green-juicing-diet

http://tinyurl.com/healthy-superfoods

The author will in any way be held responsible by any reader who fails to consult the appropriate health authorities with respect to their individual health care before acting on or using any information contained herein, and neither the author or publisher of any of this information will be held responsible for errors or omissions, or use or misuse of the information.

CPSIA information can be obtained at www.ICGtesting.com
Printed in the USA
LVOW12s2242180514

386342LV00012B/330/P